MW00577547

Snippets of Love

Thoughts to warm your heart and touch your soul

Sidney Gardiner

PUBLISHING GROUP

Snippets of Love

Copyright © 2020 by Sidney Gardiner

All rights reserved

First Edition

Hardcover ISBN: 978-1-64111-221-5
Paperback ISBN: 978-1-64111-999-3
eBook ISBN: 978-1-64111-224-6

DEDICATION

Snippets of Love is dedicated to you, to you, and to you. My desire is that if you picked up this book, it would put a smile on your face, inspire you, or make you think.
May each snippet warm your heart and touch your soul.
This is a gift of love and is meant for you.
Enjoy.

FOREWORD

Sometimes when my young daughter woke up in the morning, my wife and I did not know who we were going to meet. Was it our sweet little daughter or was it the Tasmanian devil? "Taz," we would call her. That humorous nickname stuck through all these years and we still laugh about it today. I think we all have a little Taz in us. Sometimes we all struggle with anger, bitterness, anxiety, impatience, mean-spiritedness, defiance, faithlessness, harshness, or lack of restraint. This world is in turmoil in what seems to be a nonstop downward spiral; seems like we are going from one crisis to another. Our priorities, as well as our emotions get turned upside down. Whatever happened to those random acts of kindness we used to spontaneously have in our lives? We seemed to have lost our kindness and replaced it with the 'Taz' that this world draws out of us. We all go through the Taz phase. What can break us free? Sometimes it might be better for us just to go back to bed and start the day all over again. Here is a suggestion: Go back to bed and start your day all over again with this one thing – read a page or two out of *Snippets of Love*. Sit down in your favorite chair, porch swing, comfy couch, or wherever and find a quiet corner in your life and let this comforting book put you back to the "happy place" in your life.

After reading just the first few pages of *Snippets of Love,* I'm quite certain you will find words to inspire and uplift you - something special to warm your heart and touch your soul. As a pastor for many years, I believe this book would make a great subject for a Sunday sermon, marriage counseling, anger management, or just simply a reminder of some of the basics that we have lost along the way.

~Pastor Dale

INTRODUCTION

Hello and thank you for buying this book. My name is Sidney and it is my privilege to share this book with you.

I think you may agree that we live in a whack-a-doodle world and at times it seems like this world is spinning out of control. If you look around, the political scene is uncomfortable, global warming is raising its ugly head, the educational system is broken, medical costs are so expensive that people sometimes have to choose between food and medication, and the stress of trying to cope on a daily basis becomes, at times, overwhelming. It makes one wonder what went wrong along the way.

Here's what I know for sure. Change starts with one person and soon we have collective consciousness that is powerful enough to make a radical difference for the good of *all*.

My intention in writing this book was to have you take a "time out" and simply breathe. As you turn the pages, I hope you will be reminded of the basics – the basics that so many of us have forgotten because we are so busy just trying to live life.

So, curl up in your favorite reading spot, get comfy and walk with me as we explore the beauty and challenges of our whack-a-doodle world.

Soooo, let us begin…

CHAPTER 1

Kindness Snippets

It sounds so simple.

Be a heart-based person.

SIMPLY BE KIND.

We must

STOP AND THINK

**before we talk
and take responsibility for our actions.**

It's easy to be selfish

and not care about other people,

but that's not what the world needs…

The world needs love.

We can give the world
the love that it needs through

ACTS OF KINDNESS.

So be kind.

It really does matter.

Kindness:

The Medicine That Heals

Kindness
for Healing

If you suffer from depression, selfishness, or maybe an "I don't care" attitude…

TRY KINDNESS

…*your prescription for healing*

Clinical trials have been highly successful.

- It costs nothing
- It is easy to dispense
- It can be taken multiple times a day
- Even one dose a day will heal
- Cannot overdose
- Gives immediate results

Potential side effects may include some or all of the following:

- May relieve feelings of sadness
- Depression may lift
- May cause perpetual smiling
- Could find unexpected feelings of Joy, Happiness and Gratitude

CAUTION: CONTINUED USE MAY RESULT IN A POSITIVE ADDICTION.

COMPLIMENT

SOMEONE TODAY.

And really mean it

...or don't do it.

He had the winning ticket that brought him a pot of gold
All your troubles will be over, at least that's what he was told

So, he bought the big house and fancy cars galore
It just wasn't enough, so he bought more and more

But alas, when he would go to bed sad at night
Something told him, this just isn't right

He had all this money, but unwilling to share
On some level he knew this just wasn't fair

So, he started a foundation to give it away
And the next morning woke up to a brand-new day

Money is a gift to be shared with the poor
Only then will you have joy at the heart of your core

He's happy and finally smiling at last
His selfish ways are a thing of the past

So, share what you have with those who have less
And at the end of the day you will truly be blessed

GIVE GENEROUSLY TO OTHERS.

You will grow as a person when you give to others from your heart.

Whatever way you help someone, you will get

more joy from giving

than receiving.

RECIPE FOR
SPREADING BROTHERLY LOVE

In a large bowl, combine the following ingredients:

1 cup of Kindness

½ cup of Forgiveness

2 tbsp of Understanding

3 cups of Love

½ tsp of Hope

½ tsp of Humility

½ tsp of Compassion

Gently whisk until well blended. Shape into balls with loving and gentle hands and place onto a large cookie sheet greased with the desire to serve. Bake for 30 minutes at 350°. Test with a toothpick to see if the world is ready to receive. Serve generous pieces to all those souls less fortunate and hungry for gifts from the heart.

Serving size: Can feed multitudes

I saw a homeless man walking down the street

He was tattered and torn from his head to his feet

I threw him a mental stone...
"How could you be such a mess?"
It wasn't very kind of me, I must confess

We judge and we stare and throw our hands in the air
You're not my problem, so I really don't care

But deep in my heart a little voice said,
"You must help this man now or he may soon be dead"

So, I gave him some money, thought it might help him cope
He simply nodded a thank you with eyes that said hope.

SPREAD JOY

let's hug

Hug someone today

Hug

Noun

An act of holding someone tightly in one's arms, typically to express affection.

A SINCERE HUG CAN:

- ✓ Comfort someone who is sick
- ✓ Bring a smile to a face
- ✓ Replace despair with hope
- ✓ Say I'm sorry
- ✓ Calm a sad friend
- ✓ Soothe a lonely soul
- ✓ Stop a crying child
- ✓ Fill a void in someone's heart

So, be a good hugger!

Do it often and mean it.

Go now and hug somebody...
It will make you both smile.

You would think that all hugs are the same
But some are strong, and some are lame

A hug is a gesture of affection and love
So, welcome the hug as a gift from above

The person was inspired to give you a squeeze
So, hug them back as hard as you please

Say Thank you, I needed that, you made my day
I'll pass the hug on as I go about my way
Silently saying, I did it, Hooray!

People are often unreasonable and self-centered
FORGIVE THEM ANYWAY

If you are kind, people may accuse you of ulterior motives
BE KIND ANYWAY

If you are honest, people may cheat you
BE HONEST ANYWAY

If you find happiness, people may be jealous
BE HAPPY ANYWAY

The good you do today may be forgotten
DO GOOD ANYWAY

Give the world your best and it may not be good enough
GIVE YOUR BEST ANYWAY

For you see, in the end it is between
YOU AND GOD

It was never between you and them anyway

~Mother Theresa

CHAPTER 2

Gratitude Snippets

Do you remember the song *"Count your Blessings"* by Irving Berlin?

> *"When I'm worried and I can't sleep*
>
> *I count my blessings instead of sheep*
>
> *And I fall asleep*
>
> *counting my blessings"*

Even if you do not know the song, read the words again, because that one little verse says it all.

Gratitude is the reason
for a life well lived
or a life of regrets.

It's a genuine emotion
expressing appreciation for something
or someone.

Gratitude is an inner feeling generated
from within that is an
affirmation of goodness.

GRATITUDE
CHANGES THE COURSE OF YOUR LIFE

The competitive call of money, the need to achieve and always excel at all costs is like a virus that permeates our entire being. It often makes us corrupt, a-moral, and willing to sell our soul for money. Eventually that virus can destroy lives.

The truth is money doesn't buy happiness, contentment or bring joy. It only captures the need and desire to have more, and the cycle begins. You are stuck and it's hard to break that cycle. You need to take time out and rethink your path. Then Take Action.

The daily stress of living drowns out the whispers of love and thankfulness that should be our truth.

We might have the misconception that in order to be thankful, we count only the big stuff. But the truth is, **it is the everyday little things that we acknowledge that starts the path of change in our life.**

When positive thoughts replace the whiny negative thoughts, there is an energy shift that occurs.

You are happier, your self-esteem improves, you smile more. You will find you have more appreciation for people, and when you thank them for helping you in some way, their confidence goes up and they are happier. When you are attentive and really listen to what people say, and you are grateful for their friendship or their help, it changes you and them.

Thankfulness is as simple as a great cup of coffee or as insightful as knowing you helped someone with a hug or kind word.

So, Count Your Blessings...

Start a Gratitude Journal – write in it every night before bed...

Say **"Thank You"** more to family, friends, co-workers, and strangers you meet...

Even in tough times, find something to be grateful for and write it down...

Go to sleep at night reciting a list of things that happened that day that made you say, "Wow! Thank You!"...

Have an **"Attitude of Gratitude."** You will feel the shift that will change your life... I guarantee it.

Thank you

Happiness is not from the material things…
the big house, the fancy car, money in the bank…

It is from finding your joy by giving to others…
Making a difference in someone's life…
Making the world a little better than it was before.
That's happiness. ***That is True Joy.***

Happiness is an attitude.
It is the framework of a life well lived.

Strive always to seek your joy and you
will discover happiness and peace.

Dear God,

If you would have made me **perfect**,

maybe I would **not** feel like:

…Sometimes you have forgotten about me – you just don't hear my prayers

…Sometimes you let me hurt and cry

…Sometimes I simply stop praying

But then you do something to show me your unconditional love and then I am okay again knowing you love me after all.

Even though

I'm far from perfect

For that,

I thank you.

CHAPTER 3

Love Snippets

L O V E
The Foundation of All Humanity

Wow! What a powerful statement.

Let's think about it for a minute.

Nothing stands the test of time like a strong foundation.

Then layer upon layer, a structure is built,
a relationship is formed, a marriage survives,
children grow up, companies are built.

**Love is that profound and powerful emotion
that becomes the glue to form that foundation.**

It is timeless.

This universal connection of love
impacts society on multiple levels.

Think about
all the countries of the world,
the different races,
cultures & ideologies,
and realize there is one
common denominator:

LOVE

is a beautiful word...

Soft and warm to the ear.

Love is an all-inclusive word.

We all seek love:

> *Love of a higher being,*
>
> *Love of parents,*
>
> *Love of your spouse,*
>
> *Love of family and friends,*
>
> *Love of country.*

And we love the simple things: an ice cream cone, a holiday, rainy days, and snowflakes. We love good health, and the sight of the flag flying.

All these things enrich our lives. Love creates a tapestry of life that connects us all on some level. That love brings hope to the world.

Have you ever tried to define love?

Close your eyes for a minute and think about
what love means to you.

It encompasses many factors. You might have an energetic
connection with someone. You feel lighter, happier, and safer.
You should feel kindness, compassion, respect, commitment, and
selflessness. It embodies a kind of truth. Love has an emotional
connection. It is lasting and endures time and the disappointments
of life.

Love can heal a heart or break a
heart.

Love can transform a person's life.

Love can bring hope and heal the
world.

Love can fill a void of loneliness.

Love can soothe a child.

Love gives confidence,
encouragement, and strength.

Love from a mother can change the
course of a life.

LACK of love Can And Will
Destroy.

So, Look for Love.

It surrounds us daily.

Love is...

The sunrise and sunset, beauty of the sky
Mountains, and hills, a look in the eye
Laughter, a touch, a smile sincere
These are the things we hold so dear

So, stop and listen, just look around
You will see it, touch it, and hear it's sound
Love is everywhere if you just look and see
It connects all of us – you and me

From rivers and streams and oceans so blue
We see the beauty of love shining through
Don't be a stranger, let me take your hand
We are connected through love, all over this land

And sometimes things get tough...

Life tumbled us sorrow and burdens to bare
But we held tight to each other with the love that we share
We marched hand in hand through this journey called life
Fighting battles of disappointments, sadness and strife

Through the clouds there is sunshine
And through darkness is light
Love in your heart gives you courage to fight
We'll be stronger and better, joined at the hip
Our love will survive every little dip

Often - because Love kept you together - you get to the other side

Fun and laughter, Let the good times roll
We were down, but we're back, Healed and now whole
Life is a mixture of sunshine and rain
In with the happiness, out with the pain
We're on a new path filled with goodness and light
Long days of sunshine, not a dark, lonely night

Love gives us positive energy to bounce back

Our thoughts create our life in store
Think positive and clear and you'll have more
The time has come for you to see
This is our year, BELIEVE it will be

Love is kind of hard to define

What is love? Do we even know?
It's easy to say, harder to show
A look, a smile, a tender touch
Those are the things we love so much

You will see Love – if you just look

Laughter, love and quiet hours
Beauty, songs and fragrant flowers
Cares and problems left behind
A happy heart, true peace of mind

So, my dear friend, remember this:

IF YOU WANT MORE LOVE – GIVE MORE LOVE.
It is What The World Needs Now – more than ever!

Like the beautiful song *"What The World Needs Now"* by Burt Bacharach . . . I believe says it all:

"What the world needs now is love, sweet love
It's the only thing that there's just too little of...
What the world needs now is love, sweet love
No not just for some, but for everyone..."

Life takes you to unexpected places...
Love brings you back home

~Melissa McClone

Love in your heart
wasn't put there to stay...

Love isn't love
till you give it away

~Oscar Hammerstein

LOVE LESSONS I'VE LEARNED:

If you love someone and they are not there when you need them, it will never work. Let go of that person. In the end, you will be glad that you did.

Don't compare yourself with others. There will always be someone smarter, prettier, richer, thinner. It is self-defeating. You are perfect the way you are. Learn the knack of Self-Love.

Be a reflection of what you would like to see in others.
If you want love, give love
If you want honesty, give honesty
If you want respect, give respect
Remember, you get back what you give out.

If you are looking for that person that is a perfect "10," know that they do not exist.

If you start with a foundation of shared values, morals, ethics, and life goals… You are on the right track.

Good relationships don't just happen, it takes time, patience, affection, attention and appreciation. If that person can completely turn your world upside down, then they are quite perfect for you.

When you LOVE
What you HAVE

Then you have
everything you need

Always
Remember:

You are...

Braver than you believe

Stronger than you seem

Smarter than you think

Loved more than you know

~ A.A. Milne, Winnie the Pooh

CHAPTER 4

Encouragement Snippets

10 RULES FOR A HAPPY LIFE

1. Be grateful for the big things as well as the little things

2. Believe in a higher power

3. Be kind to yourself and others – Kindness matters

4. Know your strengths and weaknesses

5. Learn what unconditional love means and practice it

6. Be true to yourself-be authentic

7. Trust your own instincts

8. Be generous with your time and money. Be a heart-based person

9. Take risks – enjoy the challenge

10. Have a positive attitude. Our thoughts control our destiny

I believe that we are who we choose to be.

Nobody is going to come and save you.
You have to save yourself.

Nobody is going to give you anything.
You have to go out and fight for it.

Nobody knows what you want, except you.

Nobody will be as sorry as you if you don't get it.

Do not be one of those wounded, weary hearts wrestling with unsolved mistakes.

Success requires a deep and compelling commitment to succeed.

You must desire this above all else.

So,

DON'T

QUIT!

Do Not Ever Give Up Your Dreams!

Think

POSITIVE ENERGY
will affect everyone around you.

(Likewise, so will negative energy)

Always

DO THE RIGHT THING.

There are No gray areas.

It is either

RIGHT

or

WRONG

It really is that simple.

Don't ever mistake

...my silence
for ignorance

...my calmness
for acceptance

...or my kindness
for weakness

~Dalai Lama

DON'T BE AFRAID

You create your own fear

You did not come into this world with fears

FACE YOUR FEARS

and then move on

HOPE

SWEET

HOPE

~Author Unknown

Life hurts sometimes.

Dig deep to find your strength
...Then Move Forward

Sometimes the

HARDEST Thing

And the

RIGHT Thing

ARE THE SAME

~Author Unknown

Everything You Want

is on

the other side

of FEAR.

~George Addair

Never Stop
Believing in HOPE
Because
Miracles Happen
Every Day

~Helen Barry

When times are tough & your future looks bleak
and you're not getting the answers that you
desperately seek

When funds are low and bills are high
Stop and cast your eyes to the sky

Say a prayer for help, God is forever near
He will never let you down, He will always hear

Trust and surrender, then do your best
God will help you with ALL of the rest

Believe in something

BIGGER

Than Yourself

Do not just have a career or a job...

Have a vocation

You are not defined by

how much money

You Have

but rather

what kind of person

You Are

Don't Be Afraid of Change

Change Forces You to Grow and Learn

Trust Your Own Decisions

You May Lose Something Good, but Find Something Better

Choose
to be

Awesome

"I have the power within to accomplish anything I want"

If you do not like the path you are on,

STOP

BREATHE

Start walking in

a new direction.

The sacrifice will be worth it.

No one else can sing your song
No one else can dance your dance
No one else can write your play

You are in charge of your destiny and your life

So, go ahead...

Sing the way you want

Dance the way you want

Write the way you want

Take control
You have the power
The next move is up to you

Sometimes the lyrics of a song ring so true.
Like this one by Lee Ann Womack. It is worth a read:

I HOPE YOU DANCE

I hope you never lose your sense of wonder
You get your fill to eat but always keep that hunger
May you never take one single breath for granted
God forbid love ever leave you empty handed

I hope you still feel small when you stand beside the ocean
Whenever one door closes, I hope one more opens
Promise me that you'll give faith a fighting chance
And when you get the choice to sit it out or dance
I hope you dance
I hope you dance

I hope you never fear those mountains in the distance
Never settle for the path of least resistance
Livin' might mean takin' chances, but they're worth takin'
Lovin' might be a mistake, but it's worth makin'

Don't let some hellbent heart leave you bitter
When you come close to sellin' out, reconsider
Give the heavens above more than just a passing glance
And when you get the choice to sit it out or dance
I hope you dance

~Lee Ann Womack

When you
are happy
you
ENJOY
the music,

When you
are sad
you
UNDERSTAND
the lyrics.
~Frank Ocean

CHAPTER 5

Coping Snippets

ANGER Kills...
people, relationships, hopes and dreams

Anger. What a wasted emotion. We all know someone who is angry. We say something like, "he has a hot temper," or "he has a short fuse," or "he's always blowing off." But what is behind it?

I believe is comes down to this: The world is a tough place to live and we are angry. Some of us more than others, and some of us act it out more than others. But the bottom line is, we're angry.

We are angry at someone, but don't know who.

We are angry at something, but don't know what.

Life's little difficulties causes us stress and anxiety. Things like getting stopped at a red light when you're already late for work, or your toast burns and that is your on-the-go breakfast. It starts as a small irritant and builds. Then, before long, it creates a ripple effect and we find ourselves at a tipping point and we lose it.

We explode.

BOOM!

You blow up, snap at your spouse, yell at the dog, you make a snarky comment to a co-worker, you slam a door, you walk with your head down, you never smile, you don't say Hi, you're just plain angry.

But it doesn't have to be that way. You can dispel anger. You can fix it. Anger can be controlled and tempered. It's not easy and it takes a conscious effort and a deliberate action plan. But it can be done.

So, if you are that angry person, filled with rage and living in fear because it could erupt at any time, here are some things you can do:

BREATHE.
Seriously. Stop and breathe.
Breathe through your nose –
smell the roses
Out through your mouth – blow
out the candles
Do this several times
Get Centered

Take a "TIME OUT" before
you speak. It's easy to say
something you will regret.

When you feel yourself in
stressful situations during the
day, short quiet times can clear
your head

Identify Positive Solutions
FOCUS ON SOLUTIONS
rather than what made you
angry

EXERCISE
Physical exercise can help
reduce stress
Go for a walk or head to the
gym

Use "I" statements so you don't
place blame
Say, "I am upset with you
because…"

Don't Hold Grudges
LEARN TO FORGIVE
Forgiveness is powerful

USE HUMOR
Try to defuse the situation by
laughing, or at least try to
lighten up

TRY MEDITATION
Learn to meditate
Try deep breathing exercises
Have a mantra that you say over
and over when you're angry
Try writing in a journal
Listen to music

GET HELP
Seek counseling if you need
help

Remember...

Don't spend another minute being angry. It can consume you and keep you stuck in the muck.

Dig deep. Find your strength and realize whatever made you angry is now over.

Commit and be ready to change your attitude.

Do not let that person or situation have power over you any longer. Take control. Now.

Close the door and FORGIVE. You will then start to heal.

You will not punish someone else by being angry. But rather you will punish and destroy yourself by holding onto the anger.

Let it go. Be free. Forgive yourself.

Be patient with yourself. Be kind to yourself.
It's a process, but you will heal.
Do it now. I know you can.

LET GO OF ANGER

Anger is self-serving and will destroy your soul.

So, when anxiety and fear grab you:

DON'T PANIC
DON'T BE SCARED

Say to yourself:

I am strong.
Everything will be alright
I am a good person
I am safe
I do good things
I have a heart full of love
The world is full of good people
Only fear can hold me back
I am not afraid
I am NOT afraid

just breathe

LONELINESS
The forgotten souls

Loneliness. That heart-wrenching cry that resonates deep from the pit of your stomach.

Listen. Do you hear it? Soft at first, then louder and louder. Soon it's blaring. You can't turn it down or off. It's a moan, a sob that screams out in the darkness. "I'm alone. I'm alone. Can anyone hear me? Please God, Make it Stop! Please. Make it Stop."

It robs you of your inner light and joy and replaces it with a darkness that overshadows each moment. We were born to be loved and nurtured, to be in tribes with social connections and bonds.

Loneliness is everywhere. It lingers in a space just beneath despair. Stop for a moment. Look around. You will see the face of loneliness everywhere. Some obvious. Some not... The lost souls in a nursing home, the folks forgotten in hospital beds, those divorced and still wondering "WHY?", Saturday night without a date, a cell phone that doesn't ring... Then there are those who seem to have it all. Good job, good looks, outgoing personality, perfect life – but really, it's just a cover; a carefully played out façade with the same soul-sucking cry of aloneness.

Loneliness swallows every ounce of hope and any happiness left behind. After a while you are simply too numb to feel the pain.

So, if I am talking to you, my friend, stay with me a little longer. I can't stop your pain. I can't give you a hand to hold or a shoulder to cry on, or the warm body to snuggle with… but let's try to see the positive side.

Think about this:

Solitude is food for the soul.

**You don't have the distractions
of the world outside.**

So just be calm and quiet for a moment.

Let the stillness wash over you.

**In the stillness
you learn, you grow, you listen.**

**The quietude transcends you to a new
level of awareness and personal growth.**
Embrace the tranquility and peace.

DON'T FIGHT IT.

It's better to be Alone and Lonely
Than be with Someone and Alone

FORGIVENESS
THE ULTIMATE PATH TO FREEDOM

This is about my discovery of the three little words, "I Forgive You." It happened many years ago, but the memory is there like it was yesterday. Some things you never forget and maybe there's a reason why you never do forget.

Forgiveness. Now that's a really tough one. It's easy to say "I forgive you" – they are only words. But those words, without feelings and emotions attached to it, are nothing more than empty space. So how do we forgive someone and why should we? Let's explore that concept for a little bit. So, I'm hoping you're still curled up and cozy because I'm going to rock the boat a bit. I'm going to ask you to think of something unpleasant, but trust me, there's a purpose and it's worth it. So, let's go ahead…Close your eyes and think of a person or situation that hurt you, that broke you, that devastated you. That sucker punch from which the depths of hurt felt like you just couldn't breathe. Now hold on to that thought for a bit…

Abuse hurts and it comes in many forms. Physical, of course, but there's also the emotional, verbal and mental. And if you happen to be someone's victim who is a master of abuse, you're in a very, very bad spot. Abuse is real and unfortunately many suffer in silence. Of course, most of us have been spared this cruel cry. Be thankful. Here's the thing, if you've never been abused in any form, you cannot possibly comprehend the fear, the desperation, the pain, that one goes through. It is unbearable and you are literally trapped. No matter how intelligent you are, how many degrees you have, how rich or poor you are, the emotions are the same, the results are the same. Abuse does not discriminate. It's a male abusing a female, it can be parents abusing children, women abusing men, workplace abuse… well, you know, it's endless.

The question I always have is . . . why do people feel it is okay to do whatever they want to harm another human being and why in our society do we allow it? Fundamentally it's wrong. The abuser knows it's wrong and yet it continues.

Now think about forgiving that person – it's almost unimaginable. The hurt is so deep, so profound, it has impacted your life in such dramatic ways, that saying, "I forgive you" and truly feeling it seems impossible. But the truth is . . . Forgiveness is the only thing that will set you free. Your abuser doesn't suffer, they don't know your pain, your heartache, only you do. And the cry is deep in your soul.

So, how do you overcome this black fog? Do you simply say, "I forgive you"? There's no CliffsNotes™ you can read, there's no course you can take, there's no church with a sermon: "Here's how you forgive." They tell you TO forgive, but they don't tell you HOW. It must come from a place deep in your heart. You have to reach a point where you say, with total conviction, "I FORGIVE YOU."

When you do, **your life will change**. You cannot and will not forget, but the pain will start to subside. It's a process. In the end, having peace of heart and peace of soul will be worth it.

I have forgiven people in my life and it wasn't easy. Once you forgive, there is an emotional shift that takes place. You no longer look at that person or situation that hurt you in the same way. It's not gone…It's not forgotten, but it's okay. We all make mistakes. God made us human after all. Don't we all deserve a second chance? It's up to you to find the strength; the belief that forgiveness can and will heal.

Forgiveness is the ultimate unselfish gift of love.

In life we make decisions all day, every day. From having your morning Starbucks to navigating through traffic, to work decisions, family decisions – it's an all day long constant.

So, now I'm asking you to make one of the biggest decisions of your life.

Will you forgive the person that broke you in so many ways?

Will you finally have peace?

Will you finally have freedom?

Will you finally let go of the anchor drowning you in despair?

YOU MUST DECIDE.
It's your choice.

I did and now I'm at peace.
I hope, for your sake,
you make the right decision
and forgive.
It will set you free at last.

He hit me so hard I fell to the ground
I was stunned and bleeding when I heard the sound

His words were saying, You are worthless to me
You ruined my life don't you see

Through the tears I suddenly saw the gun
All I could think of was run, baby, run

I tried getting up, but he pushed down again hard
The front door was close, maybe a yard

I fled for my life and was safe at last
This will be a memory deep in my past

Days turned to months, months to a year
I couldn't get over my anguish and fear

So, I called him one day told him we need talk
When I met him, I said let's go take a walk

I looked him in the eye and with conviction so true
Said I'm telling you now, I'm forgiving you
He started to cry and with honest remorse in his eyes
Said thank you for forgiving me, I'm sorry too

So, the lesson, my friend, for you to see
Is that saying "I FORGIVE YOU" can set you free

REGRETS:
WOULD HAVE...COULD HAVE...SHOULD HAVE

If you're honest with yourself, I'm sure you will admit to a life sprinkled with REGRETS. For some, a few and with others it is more like a laundry list; the relentless wrestling with unsolved mistakes.

Regrets are like a sticky residue
that gets stuck in your brain.

Lost in your aloneness, it's tormenting. When you do something against your better judgment, regrets will eat away at you, one bite at a time. Eventually leaving a permanent stain.

It's like an emotional volcano ready to erupt...always blaming others or circumstances.

Every decision ever made is based on the combination of the facts on hand and the people involved. You start to analyze every action and every decision from every angle.

You then put up the wall for protection, shielding you from feelings of guilt and shame that eventually get stuffed...leaving you ALONE. **The wall never really works for long because you know it is a lie.**

You cannot turn the clock back for a Do-Over. IT IS OVER. Can you learn from it? Sure...

Understand the regret before it becomes
permanently etched in your heart.

THERE IS ALWAYS ONE DECISION THAT CHANGED EVERYTHING.
What should I have done differently? What should I have NOT done at all?

In the end, the Biggest Regrets are ALL THE THINGS YOU COULD HAVE DONE ...BUT DIDN'T

like...

...getting that college degree
...marrying the one you dumped
...choosing not to have children
...joining the Peace Corp instead of taking the corporate ride.

Regret is not the things that you have tried and failed, like...

...starting a business
...running a marathon
...flunking that college course.

If you fail at something, analyze the problem, find another solution, change the course of action and start over.

So, how do we handle regrets?

- *Seek forgiveness. Forgive yourself. And be honest.*

- *BE TRUE TO YOURSELF.*

- *Don't chase money and sacrifice happiness.*

- *Learn to Love and Trust.*

- *Try to shake the memories of hurt and doubt.*

- *Acknowledge that we screw up sometimes…as parents, spouses, workers, friends and others. We can fix it. Don't let it fester.*

- *Some regrets are meant to help us. It's a reminder of what we never want to do or say ever again. To repeat would be too painful.*

- *Learn to forgive others. Set yourself free.*

- *If you regret you have not done enough – DO MORE.*

- *Don't regret getting older – with age we gain wisdom. Wrinkles don't matter!*

- *DON'T SELL OUT - - IT'S YOUR LIFE.*

- *Don't regret being a grumpy negative person – change and lighten up.*

Woulda-Coulda-Shoulda

The familiar tapes go round and round
Can't seem to stop the hopeless sound

We all make mistakes – I did my fair share
Regrets are too many – it's heavy to bear

I turned left – Oops, not right
Decisions, choices, moments of fright

We act on what we know at the time
What is foremost and active on our mind

Life brings happiness, sadness and pain
We have some losers, we have some gains

But a life well lived is when you can honestly say,
I did the best that I could day after day

The past is the past, it's over, it's done
So create thoughts of tomorrow – a new day in the sun

The peace you are seeking will be yours at last
If you forgive yourself first and accept your past

I tell you it's not easy – it is hard to do
Commit to start and you'll discover a new you

Dear Self:

Today is the day for new rules

No More Regrets

- ## Cut ties with friends that are toxic.
  They may mean well, but if you are around them and you don't feel good about yourself...they are toxic. Dump them. They may not understand. Do it gently...but do it.

- ## Live Life for You
  Not a spouse or partner, your children or parents...but YOU. If you fail, then so be it. But if you succeed – You Win! It's Your Life.

- ## Forgive Yourself – Be Free
  This is so important – it bears repeating: Forgive yourself – Be Free.

- ## No longer choose Money Over Happiness
  Money does not buy happiness – it pays the bills. Commit to living NOW. Don't be on your death bed with "woulda – coulda - shoulda" on your lips.

The dance with the demons goes on every night
Can't stop. I try – with all of my might

My mind keeps reliving regrets from the past
I'm haunted... Please God, give me peace at last

I cry. I pray. I do all that I know
Release the shackles – GO DEMONS GO!!

EMOTIONS:

The very thing that makes us human.
You can have happiness, love, pride,
excitement, compassion. Every emotion
considered good.

But what would you be if you didn't feel
hurt, or pain, or sadness and despair?

You cannot have the
good without the bad.

There is no light without the darkness.

**The trick is to BALANCE them so the
bad does not seem so terrible and
you can truly appreciate the good.**

"I AM PERFECT JUST THE WAY I AM"

(I didn't always believe that.)

We have all been Snookered - - The truth here is finally exposed.

So, my friend, I have a huge confession to make. **I have stopped looking for the Fountain of Youth.** Oh, I could tell you stories of my relentless quest, my seemingly endless journey to the spring waters of everlasting youth and beauty. You're probably asking yourself, why would you stop looking? The plain and simple truth is we have all been conned. It doesn't exist! But alas, what I would discover was the truth. A truth so profound and so life changing that it makes Ponce de Leon's mission look like child's play.

Oh, we've been made to believe that it does exist. I know what you're thinking…this is right up there with Santa Claus and the Easter Bunny. So now you're wondering, Sidney, how could you let us all down with such devastating news? It's true…

Ya Ain't Gonna Find It – No, Nada, Nope!

Don't think I haven't visualized this picture – I can see it now, the cover of Time magazine, Person of the Year…my flawless face smack in the center with the caption reading, *"Sidney Gardiner discovers Fountain of Youth. The human race will forever be young and beautiful."* I will, no doubt, receive the Lifetime Achievement Award. I will be in the annals of history forever. OK, Mr. de Leon, move over – I did it, not you! And some of you would say, Yes, it's true. I really met her. She's a living, breathing testimonial for the perfect, youthful vibrant female. No junk in her trunk, for sure!

I searched for the infamous fountain, the wellspring that would give everlasting life and beauty to whomever bathed or drank from its waters. Warm hope burned in my heart of regaining youthful strength and vitality, including perfect eyesight-eliminating glasses, great hair-without the help of my best friend, L'Oréal. I longed to just stick my toe in and then ever so slowly, cherishing the moment, immerse my entire body into the magical waters. Years, flaws, wrinkles, and fat… just fading away. I can feel the cool refreshing water as it washes over my tired body. I smell the crispness in the air, and the infused scent of unfamiliar fragrances. It is a moment in time, freeze framed. My transformation. My deliverance at last.

Ponce de Leon and his search was nothing compared to my quest, after all, he was a man – he didn't have as much to gain as I did. My search started out in the unchartered land of social pressure. The competitive, harsh world of having to look good. Mother Nature is not kind and time takes its toll. It was a magic vision that led me to the new shores of plastic surgeons, cosmetic dentists, the world of shapers and Spanx. I bathed in every stream that I met, led by the hope that one might hold the powers of perpetual youth, and in which depths I was quite sure the dream of enhancement would be found. Marvelous healing properties would be coursing through my veins. Somewhere among the tide of anti-aging 21st Century miracles, I would discover the true Fountain of Youth.

But, alas, the truth most be told. I have a secret and perhaps – I'm just saying – that maybe the mystery lies in a much deeper crevasse of our mind. Not at all plunging in life-giving waters…

Months passed, and months turn into years. The search continued. But a newfound shore of enlightenment is surfacing. Self-Help books, seminars, classes…a new picture is starting to form in my mind's eye.

Could self-awareness, confidence, self-esteem, loving yourself possibly be more important than youth and beauty? Bringing to you an inner and outer peace and beauty at last? I found the answer to be a firm and definite YES!

The path of loving and accepting yourself is painful and is hard work, but the end result – once you've walked over the hot coals and reached the other side – is TRUE JOY.

You realize you are perfect in every way
and that your light shines bright
and that you do have the power
to inspire and influence others
and shine in ways that are a positive example.

So, my friend, be the light - the light that shines kindness, compassion, and love. Then when you look in the mirror you will see a new beautiful person. Screw Ponce de Leon. He didn't have a clue!

So. **LET'S TAKE THIS PLEDGE NOW.** Place your right hand over your heart and repeat after me (OK – so pretend I'm there):

> *I solemnly swear to stop looking for the "Fountain of Youth."*
>
> *I accept and understand that it does not exist.*
>
> *I realize that with every wrinkle, I have learned a valuable life lesson.*
>
> *I know that with every laugh line, I smiled at something that warmed my heart.*
>
> *I realize that my belly fat, love handles, and bouncing butt teaches me self-love and acceptance.*
>
> *I hereby, today, embrace all my flaws and imperfections, because I know God made me perfect, just the way I am. And God doesn't make mistakes.*
> *So – help – me – Sidney!*

CHAPTER 6

Destiny Snippets

DESTINY

A lot of us think that what controls our destiny in life are things like education, where we were born, what race we are, who our parents are, how much money we have. But that's not true.

Perhaps you think that what you say, what words come out of your mouth, determine your life. But that's not it.

What in fact controls our life, our path, our destiny… what we choose in life… are the tape recordings that constantly play in our head. All the little words that you whisper to yourself every day. Those are the words that have the power to control the outcome of your life. Words like:

You are successful
You are a failure
You can do it
Why are you so stupid?
See, you messed up again
What a great accomplishment

It's these little tapes – that "little voice in your head," as we call it, that plays those words over and over again.

The messages gather strength and power and impact us on a subconscious level. These messages can be positive or negative. They can create a better life or destroy a life.

So be careful.
Control your thoughts. Because your thoughts control you.

Be deliberate in what you think,
so that your thoughts create a positive, successful, happy life.

It takes practice and it's not easy, but you can do it.
I know you can.

When you trust
and surrender
You will see...

God will be ALL
that you need
Him to be

The Dirty Little Lies That Mess With Our Head

This is Jenny's story. Could it be something like yours?

I was walking down the street with my two best friends – Low Self-Esteem and Poor Decisions. As I turn the corner, I can see my house. I open the gate and with my eyes cast down, I nod a hello to my two roommates (Mom and Dad). My soulmates hear me and about knock me over with sloppy kisses. My black lab named BadAss and my brown and white cocker named Whiny Little Bitch love me, I'm quite sure of that. I have on a black tank top and yoga pants. The yoga pants say yoga class, but the butt inside those pants screams McDonalds. I make my way to my 8x10 hide-a-way and flop on my unmade bed with crumbled up sheets and blankets. I have barely laid my head on the pillow when the old tapes start repeating the worn-out messages: *Why am I such a loser? My life sucks.* In the safety of my aloneness, the tears start. My tears are flooding my heart with sadness. They represent my aching soul. There is no past, no future, only the present. Just Now. And it hurts beyond words. In my diary I have created a character and a voice to escape my self-doubting and hopeless thoughts. I write, *I am not a victim of abusive parents, I have not been dumped by my fiancé two weeks before the wedding, I did not flunk two of my college courses, I am not back home living with the two that started my self-doubts in the first place. I am not alone in the world. I am not weary.* But the diary was a lie because it was all true. I was the paragon of a confused human being. Half of my life fantasy (what I longed to be) and half nightmare (Reality). My cry was deep.

Let's explore WHY Jenny's life did not go as she planned or expected.
Perceptions = Reality

Myth #1:

Your success or happiness is determined by parents, race or privileged lifestyle

Actually, that is False.

This passage from Jeff Olson, I believe, says it all:

"Every day in every moment you get to exercise choices that will determine whether or not you will be a great person living a great life. Greatness, success is not something predetermined, predestined or carved into your fate by forces beyond our control. Greatness and success are always in the moment of decision."

Myth #2:

Failure means Loser

False! Failure is absolutely necessary to achieve success. If you are working on a project, no matter what it is . . . personal, or business, and it simply falls apart and no longer yields a positive outcome – STOP – Breathe – Rethink. Start a new action plan. You are not a loser. You are brilliant for recognizing that it's not working, so move on.

Myth #3:

I don't have all the degrees to succeed

Wrong. Get passionate about your project or goal. Pour your heart and soul into it. Determine your "WHY" and stick to it. Perseverance will overcome the lack of degrees. The definition of perseverance is "persistence in doing something despite difficulty or delay in achieving success."

Myth #4:

I'm stuck because I need lots of money to move on

The fact is most people start small. Rent a room if you can't afford an apartment. Take one college course instead of a full load. Work two jobs if you need to but stay on track with your conviction to move your life forward. No matter what.

Myth #5:

My parents abused me, so I'm damaged goods and worthless
Let's face it, we are all a product of our parent's beliefs, behaviors and actions. But it stops there. We have control as an adult, even as a teen. You must realize a simple fact of life: Maybe it was wrong, abusive, unloving, but unfortunately statistics show that a large percentage of adults come from dysfunctional families/ parents.

SO, YOU MUST:
- recognize the behavior
- change your perception
- create a new reality
- stay strong with your own convictions
- accept the truth

Your parents do not define you. You can change.
Have the strength to forgive.
Have faith in a higher being.
Move in a new direction.
ONE STEP AT TIME.

The wheel will start to turn, and a new vision will guide you to newfound success and happiness.

Did I mention PEACE?
Maybe our sad little Jenny will be free at last.

Your Past Shapes You

But Does Not Define You

Success is not final
Failure is not fatal

It is the

COURAGE TO CONTINUE

that really counts.
*That's what makes the
difference.*

~Winston Churchill

YOU HAVE GOT THREE CHOICES IN LIFE:

1 Give Up

2 Give In, or

3 Give it all You've Got

~Charleston Parker

When you are lost and can't find your way
Take a moment and stop to simply pray

When you think that God is too busy to hear
Know for a fact that He is always near

No problem is ever to big or too small
God will take time to solve them all

So, when you're troubled with a weary heart
Seek God first, then do your part

The answers will come, you will have peace at last
The problem you had will be a thing of the past

Hope knows
NO limits

Nothing happens unless you work at it.

- Set a goal
- Have an action plan
- Work your butt off
- Track your accomplishments
- Reward yourself along the way

Understand the Consequences

of Your Actions

...both good and bad

THE POWER IS WITHIN YOU

YOUR LIFE IS A BLANK CANVAS AND YOU ARE THE ARTIST

You design the life you want to live
Paint It Bold, Vibrant & Exciting
Or Paint It Soft & Subtle & Calm

YOU DECIDE

No one else can
Live the life you choose
Enjoy the journey
You designed it

ARE YOU SINCERE IN WHAT YOU WANT?

Choose this very minute.

What you can do
What you can dream
What is your true goal

- Insist on being clear and unequivocal about your intentions

- Point your life in a specific direction that resonates within you to the core

- Be bold, be firm on what you desire

- Thoughts have power and magic

- Engage the mind and then feel the emotions of your desires

Soon the law of attraction will fulfill your dreams

A LIFE WELL LIVED
IS TO DIE IN PEACE

You are always

ONE DECISION

from a totally

different

path,

so make sure you think it out carefully.

STOP LOOKING FOR HAPPINESS IN THE SAME PLACE YOU LOST IT

Your Greatest Victory
comes only after
your most painful loss

Anything and **Everything**

Is Yours . . .

For A PRICE

Make sure the price is worth it.

Live A Sustainable Life

Know your Footprint

Protect our Planet

You CAN Make a Difference

Start a grassroots movement
for change

Pick a topic that you are
passionate about

Speak Up – Speak Out –
Let Your Voice Be Heard

You Have the Power Within

Be Part of Healing Our World

CLOSING THOUGHTS:

Harmony helps you discover a whole new world of possibilities. Joyous, useful, and successful living is harmonious living.

All aspects of health: mental, physical, and spiritual are nothing more than the harmonious arrangements of the forces within your own life.

You must strive to live in harmony with yourself. If you learn the knack of creating harmony between yourself and your environment, you've discovered one of the great secrets of life.

We must live our life with purpose and function. We must have reverence and respect for our world and the environment, and the nobility of character to act on behalf of the good of all humanity in an approach to living a better, more sustainable life.

Let us call together those who desire to work in harmony for the discovery or awareness of a common goal. When applied and practiced, men and women of all races and backgrounds will unite and work as one.

I ask you, in all sincerity, have you given any thought to what you can do to help our world? Small steps will collectively help in the whole earth healing. Commit now to a pathway to a more purposeful life. The quest for a better world is no longer a luxury. It is well on its way to becoming a necessity. Because of the crisis of our time, don't wait until you find the initial spark of interest in a moment of grief or sorrow, or in some personal tragedy, or perhaps a time of pain or illness. Make a commitment now and discover an awareness and sense of fulfillment. You will never be the same. You personally will participate in whole earth harmony.

So, we come now to the end of our time together. I hope that maybe some of the words made a lot of sense to you, and some even got a "wow" or a "Yes, that's true."

What I would like you to remember and take with you is the belief that you have a responsibility to practice and remember some of the snippets you've just read...

The world needs lots and lots of love. So, remember to spread that love through Acts of Kindness and by always doing the right thing, without question.

Know that you have value as a human being and your voice can and will be heard. Be part of a whole earth harmony and healing.

You are an over-the-top amazing human being. Believe it. You have the power within you to make changes. Claim that power today.

Enjoy the journey, my friend. The world will be a better place because of you.

I am sending you love and a giant hug.

Remember, be the light - you were born to shine.

SPECIAL ACKNOWLEDGMENTS

Special thanks to Brenda Carson for her talent of formatting this book and putting life into my words using creativity with fonts and images - the best graphics gal ever. Thank you also Brenda, for your endless hours and dedication that you put into *Snippets of Love* and the patience you exhibited in dealing with me and my revisions, always with a positive attitude and smile. You are absolutely amazing, Brenda!

Illustration credits to depositphotos.com, uihere.com, and openclipart.org.

Thanks also to my friend and editor Susan Gaines for her hard work and kind words of encouragement. I appreciate your input, Susan. Thank you so much.

A very special thank you to Pastor Dale Robertson for taking time out of his very busy schedule to write the Foreword to *Snippets of Love*. His words of encouragement and hope I know will be a blessing to many.

ABOUT THE AUTHOR

 When you see the phrase "**Snippets of Love**" it is almost synonymous with Sidney Gardiner. It is a phrase that holds great meaning to the author because her kindhearted personality is a true expression of love, demonstrated by the way she lives her life. Her down-to-earth ability to connect with people and her genuine desire to help others makes Sidney stand out as a respectable leader and an authentic caregiver who spreads love wherever she goes. These are all things that contribute to her heartfelt understanding of the human experience.

Born in a small agricultural town in Michigan, Sidney was raised with a strong work ethic and a steady moral compass. After pursuing a degree in Healthcare, she confidently left the security and familiarity of home, setting out to explore the country. Sidney moved to Denver, then to Palo Alto where she enjoyed successful careers in Healthcare as an O.R. Assistant, Surgical Sales Consultant and Wellness Coach. Recently, she transitioned from the Healthcare field into Real Estate.

Sidney now resides in Parkland, Florida. It was there she shared 27 years with her husband Sonny until his recent death in March 2020. Sidney can be found doing talks at local venues and is involved in a variety of charity organizations. She enjoys the Florida lifestyle, working on stained glass projects, and, of course, her favorite pastime, writing.

Snippets of Love is the first book in a series and will soon be followed by *Snippets of Love for Caregivers* and *Snippets of Love for Grandmothers,* released by Christmas 2020. The fourth book Sidney is working on, *Till Death Do Us Part: Toxic Mold, The Silent Killer* will be released in 2021.

Visit www.snippetsoflove.com for more information.

Feel free to contact Sidney at sidney@snippetsoflove.com.

Printed in the USA
CPSIA information can be obtained
at www.ICGtesting.com
LVHW072350290823
756597LV00002B/19